Thomas'
Wonderful Word Book

Based on *The Railway Series* by the Rev. W. Awdry

CONTENTS

6-7   **AT THE STATION**

8-9   **ON THE PLATFORM: COLOURS**

10-11   **A WEEK ON SODOR**

12-13   **IN THE TOWN: LETTERS**

14-15   **ON A PICNIC: LETTERS**

16-17   **AT THE SCHOOL**

18-19   **IN THE WILDLIFE PARK**

20-21   **AT THE TOWN STATION**

22-23   **ON THE BUSY RIVER**

24-25   **AT THE FUNFAIR: COLOURS**

26-27   **IN THE COUNTRYSIDE**

28-29   **BUSY FARM LIFE**

EGMONT
We bring stories to life

This edition published in Great Britain 2005
by Egmont Books Limited
239 Kensington High Street, London W8 6SA
Illustrations by Robin Davies and Niall Harding

Thomas the Tank Engine & Friends

A BRITT ALLCROFT COMPANY PRODUCTION

Based on The Railway Series by The Rev W Awdry

© Gullane (Thomas) LLC 2005

ISBN 1 4052 2008 2
5 7 9 10 8 6
Printed in Singapore

30-31   SEASONS: SPRING AND SUMMER

32-33   SEASONS: AUTUMN AND WINTER

34-35   PICKING UP PASSENGERS: COUNTING

36-37   AT THE HARBOUR

38-39   ON THE BEACH

40-41   HAPPY ENGINES: SHAPES

42-43   ON THE FARM

44-45   OUT AND ABOUT: OPPOSITES

46-47   AT THE FAT CONTROLLER'S HOUSE

48-49   THE BIRTHDAY PARTY

50-51   TELL THE TIME: MORNING – LUNCH

52-53   TELL THE TIME: AFTERNOON – NIGHT

54-57   FUN QUIZ

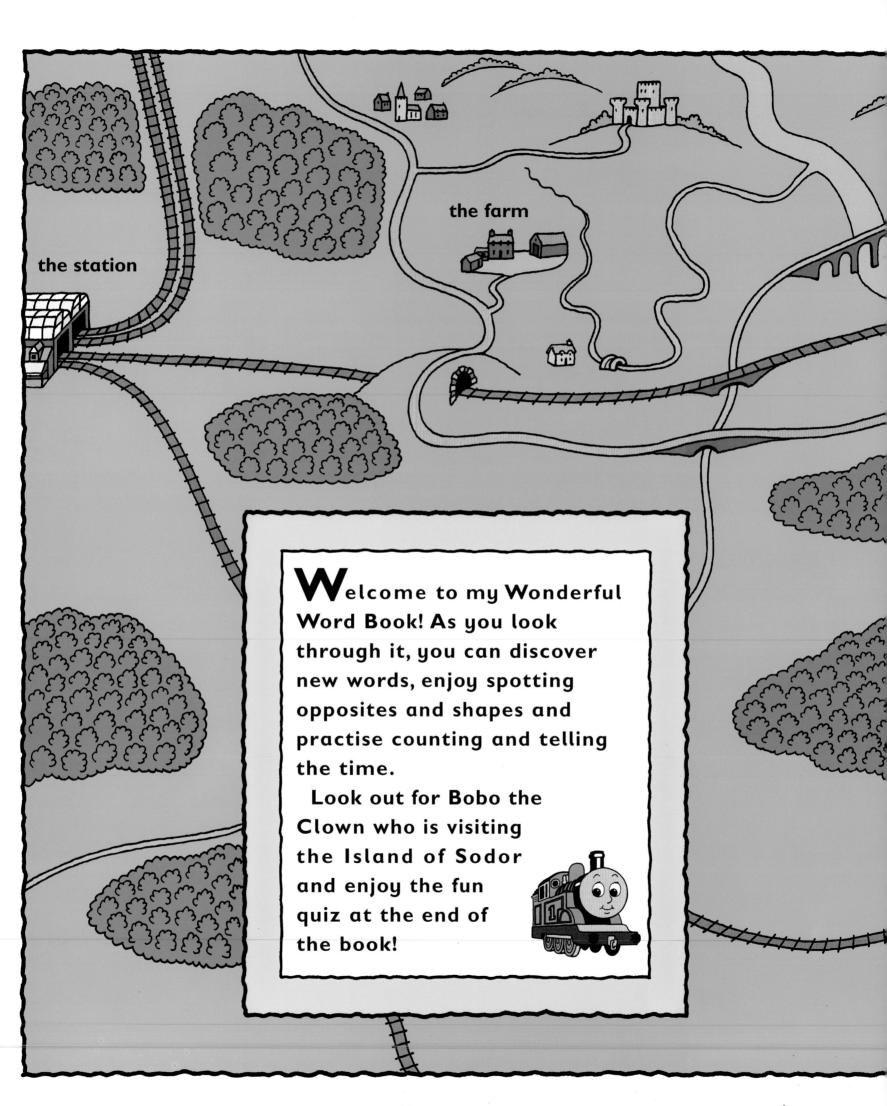

the station

the farm

Welcome to my Wonderful Word Book! As you look through it, you can discover new words, enjoy spotting opposites and shapes and practise counting and telling the time.

Look out for Bobo the Clown who is visiting the Island of Sodor and enjoy the fun quiz at the end of the book!

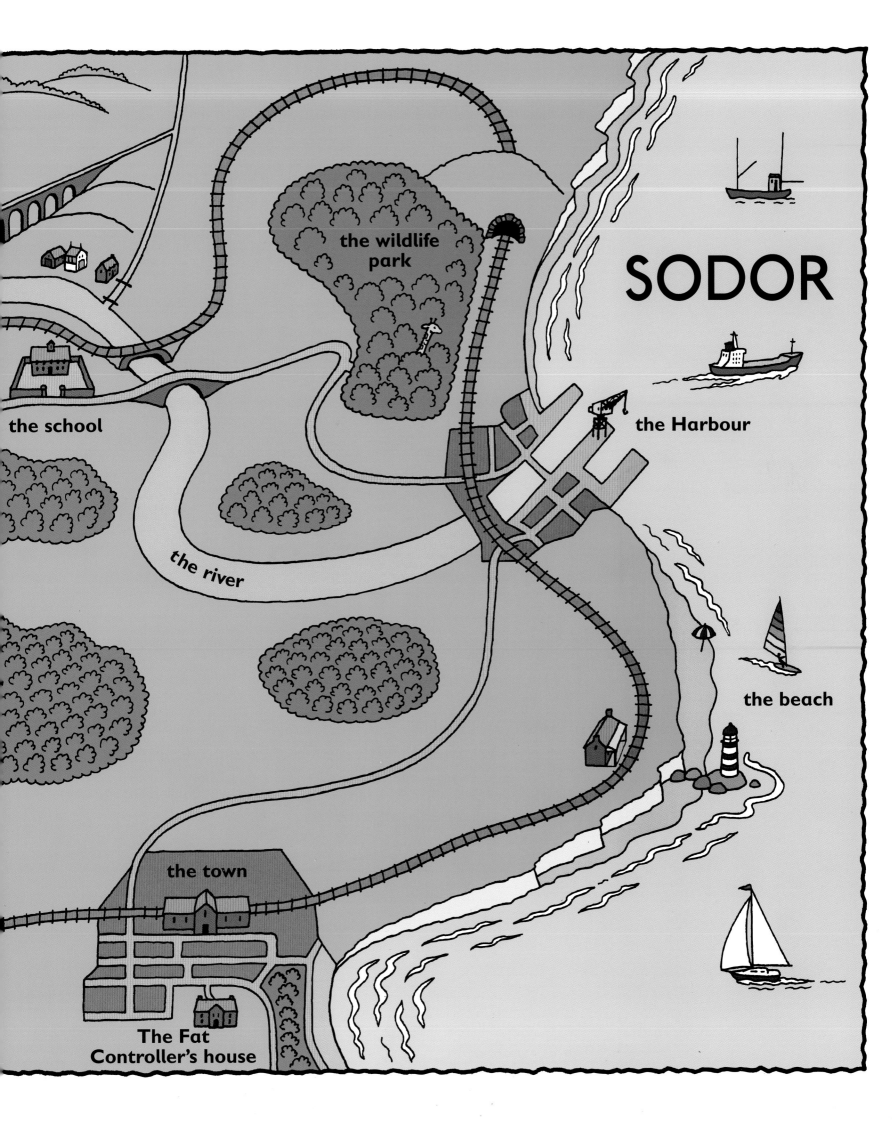

AT THE STATION

water tower

coal bunkers

Duck

Edward

siding

trucks

turntable

roof

Toby

points

signal box

buffers

signal

James

rails

Clarabel

Annie

Annie

BOBO

road

red bag

brown teddy bear

pink bucket and spade

brown suitcase

green bin

ON THE PLATFORM:

shop

Snacks/Drinks

newspaper kiosk

OPEN

be

Station master

parcels

FRAGILE

buggy

coal

Driver

1

platform

Guard

The Fat Controller

Porter

COLOURS

clock

waiting room

ticket office

TO PLATFORMS
2, 3 and 4

passenger

carriage

Annie

luggage
trolley

family

THIS WAY UP

brown briefcase

green flag

yellow umbrella

blue parcel

grey pigeon

· A WEEK ON SODOR ·

MONDAY
The Mayor gives The Fat Controller a medal for his work on the Railway.

TUESDAY
Harold flies to the Harbour.

WEDNESDAY
The Fat Controller is busy in his office.

THURSDAY
James breaks down in a tunnel.

FRIDAY

Percy gets a new coat of paint.

SATURDAY

Percy takes passengers to the town.

SUNDAY

Thomas takes children to the seaside.

a for ambulance

b for Bertie

c for camera

d for dog

e for elephant

f for fire engine

FILM

g for garage

h for hose

i for ice-cream

j for jacket

k for kitten

l for ladder

m for motor bike

n for nest

o for orange

p for picnic basket

q for queen

r for rainbow

s for sandwich

t for tree

u for umbrella

v for van

w for wheel

x for xylophone

y for yoghurt

z for zebra

AT THE SCHOOL

hamster

crayons

dinosaur

pirate hat

Thomas book

blackboard

globe

paint brushes

paintings

Spring

computer

teacher

chalk

register

desk

books

drum

fish tank

toy car

tambourine

fish food

recorder

Summer   Autumn   Winter

play house

window

doll

balloon

cupboard

blocks

train set   table

jigsaw

chair

mask   crown   cowboy hat   dressing-up box

aeroplane

pen

jigsaw piece

goldfish

apple

IN THE WILDLIFE PARK

buffalo

polar bear

penguin

kangaroo

elephant

hippopotamus

flamingo

tiger

rhinoceros

Wildlife Park

Bertie

camel

ticket office

school party

18

sea

giraffe

ostrich

panda

monkey house

lion

chimpanzee

gazelle

visitors

zebra

meerkat

19

AT THE TOWN STATION

policeman

telephone box

motor bike

washing line

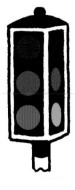

traffic lights

steeple

town hall

house

church

fire engine

driveway

car

van

shops

coach

Dan D. Lion & Son

Eat CHEESE

TOYS B US

police car

street light

road

pavement

truck

petrol pump

aerial

door

swings

pair of glasses

ON THE BUSY RIVER

aqueduct

Bulstrode

sail

yacht

BULSTRODE

fender

river bank

dinghy

police boat

POLICE

school

children

playground

wall

22

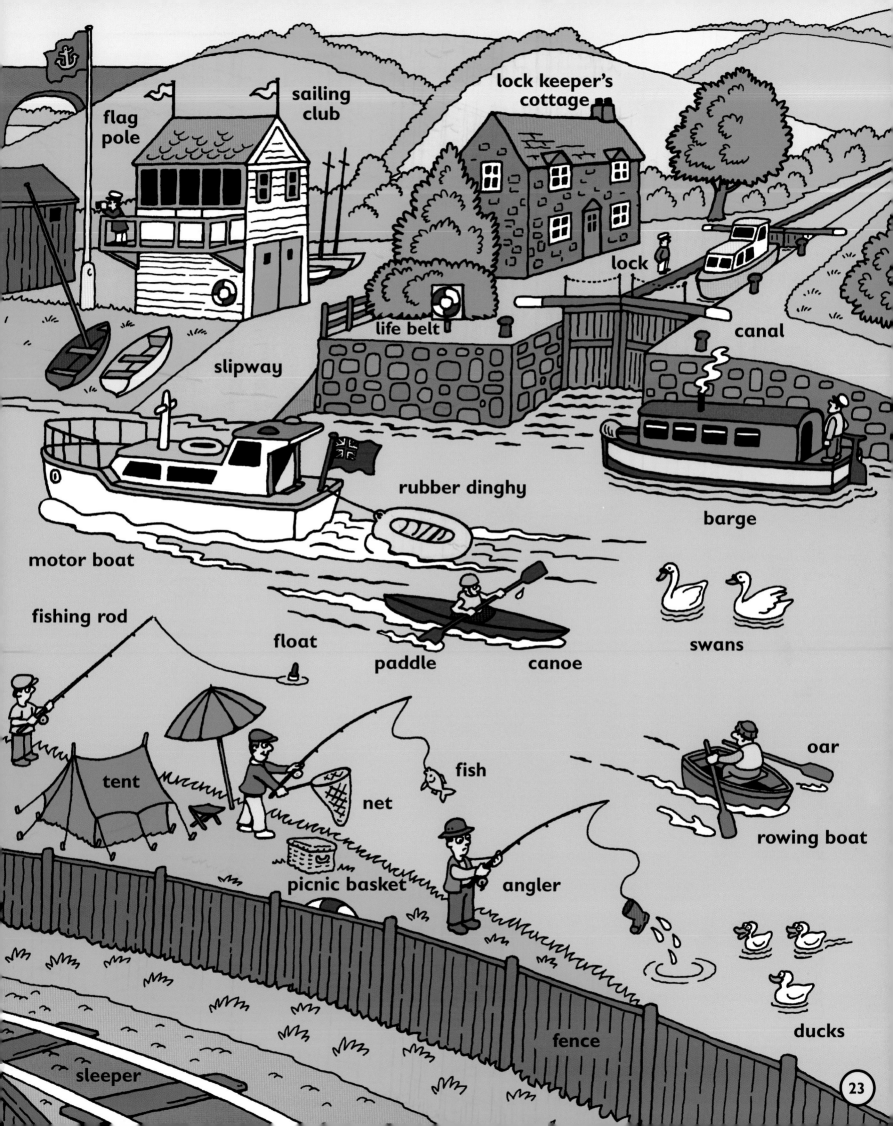

flag pole

sailing club

lock keeper's cottage

lock

canal

life belt

slipway

rubber dinghy

barge

motor boat

fishing rod

float

paddle

canoe

swans

oar

tent

fish

net

rowing boat

picnic basket

angler

fence

ducks

sleeper

23

Can you see . . .

RED Bertie?

an ORANGE jumper?

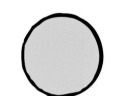

a YELLOW sun?

a GREEN flag?

a BLUE balloon?

AT THE FUNFAIR:

COLOURS

PURPLE flowers?

a BLACK hat?

BROWN
coconuts?

PINK candyfloss?

WHITE Harold?

IN THE COUNTRYSIDE

forest

corn field

Bertie

farm

grass

country lane

kestrel

cows

tunnel

badger

hedge

fox

mountain biker

sheep

Clarabel

rabbits

bird's nest

workmen

track

26

clouds

castle

hills

chimney

tree

cottage

combine harvester

scarecrow

walkers

gate

bridge

stream

Annie

funnel

flowers

spade

track

27

piglet

thrush

lamb

bull

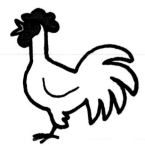

cockerel

• BUSY FARM LIFE •

Terence

farm house

pigsty

stable

cat

boots

axe

milk churn

farmer

straw bale

horse

goat

cattle grid

hedgehog

aystack

barn

robin

ewe

ram

sheepdog

hen house

donkey

log

barrel

chicken

Trevor

farm truck

pond

ducks

chicks

cows

calf

sparrow

29

SEASONS: SPRING AND SUMMER

SPRING
James rides through the farm in the pouring rain.

SUMMER

Percy waits in the Harbour. It's lovely and sunny there.

SEASONS: AUTUMN AND WINTER

AUTUMN

The school children wave at Thomas as he goes by. It is getting colder and the leaves are falling off the trees.

star

Henry

tinsel

fir tree

gloves

shovel

scarf

snow

boots

snowballs

sledge

robin

holly

skates

ice

snowman

WINTER

Henry watches the children playing. It's fun to slide about in the snow!

Can you see . . .

1 clock?

2 benches?

3 newspapers?

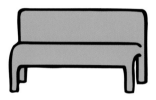

4 birds?

5 posters?

• PICKING UP PASSENGERS:

COUNTING

Can you see . . .

6 passengers?

7 mail bags?

8 suitcases?

9 parcels?

10 flowers?

crab

capstan winch

dolphin

mop

flatfish

AT THE HARBOUR

beach

crane

buoy

container

ladder

bow

container ship

diver

fish
market

fishing net

rope

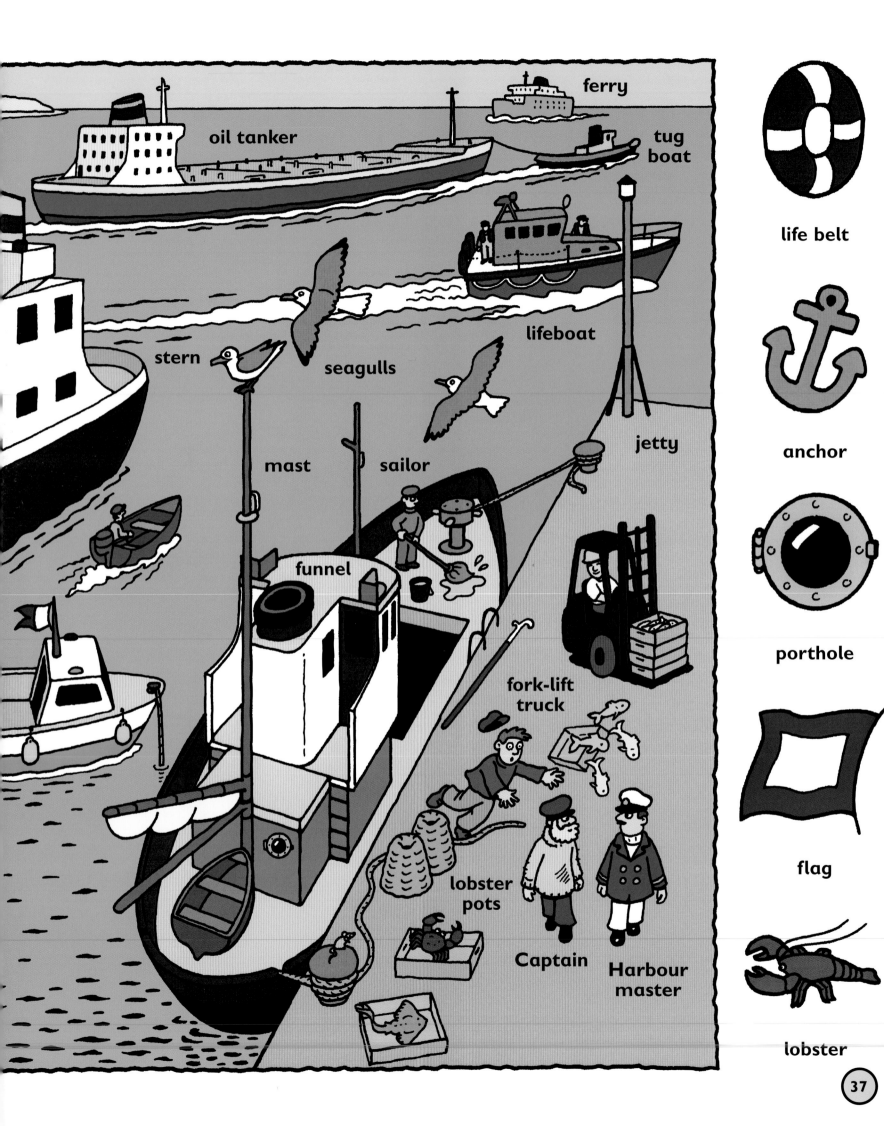

ferry

oil tanker

tug
boat

life belt

lifeboat

stern

seagulls

jetty

anchor

mast

sailor

funnel

porthole

fork-lift
truck

lobster
pots

flag

Captain

Harbour
master

lobster

Can you see . . .

a CIRCLE?

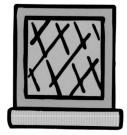

a SQUARE?

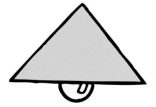

a TRIANGLE?

40

Can you see . . .

a STAR?

a DIAMOND?

a RECTANGLE?

ON THE FARM

Trevor

Terence

logs

scarecrow

stable

horse

pigs

hay

sheep

sheepdog

goat

potatoes

cauliflowers

basket

carrots

cabbages

42

Up

Down

Open

Closed

Big

Little

Over

Under

Left

Right

Asleep

Awake

BATHROOM

picture

chair

desk

tiles

taps

bath

shampoo

mirror

toilet

sink

BEDROOM

Harold

poster

blind

toy box

toys

coat stand

letter box

front door

mirror

telephone

floor tiles

vase

cushion

sofa

carpet

vacuum cleaner

LIVING ROOM

47

THE BIRTHDAY PARTY

I am 5

badge

party hat

bow

birthday present

pink shoes

birthday cake

juggling balls

clown

patio

plant pot

unicycle

steps

grass

dog

flower bed

lemonade

fairy cakes

jelly

glass

sausage rolls

jug

biscuits

cheese

table cloth

presents

table

socks

children

bouncy castle

shoes

balloons

plates

bowls

party game

blanket

spoons

blue balloon

orange juice

crisps

candles

trumpet

TELL THE TIME: MORNING – LUNCH

7 o'clock

The engines wake up at 7 o'clock.

8 o'clock

Thomas picks up his passengers at the station at 8 o'clock.

9 o'clock

At 9 o'clock, James passes by the school.

10 o'clock

Harold is flying past the Lighthouse at 10 o'clock.

11 o'clock

It's 11 o'clock and Edward arrives with some parcels.

12 o'clock

The clock strikes 12 o'clock in the town.

1 o'clock

The Fat Controller has his sandwiches at 1 o'clock.

2 o'clock

At 2 o'clock, Terence is ploughing the field.

TELL THE TIME: AFTERNOON – NIGHT

3 o'clock

Percy arrives at the Docks at 3 o'clock.

4 o'clock

The children wave goodbye to Thomas at 4 o'clock.

5 o'clock

It's 5 o'clock and Henry is going back to the engine shed.

6 o'clock

The engines have a wash at 6 o'clock.

7 o'clock

Time for bed at 7 o'clock. Goodnight!

• FUN QUIZ •

Where did we find the following?

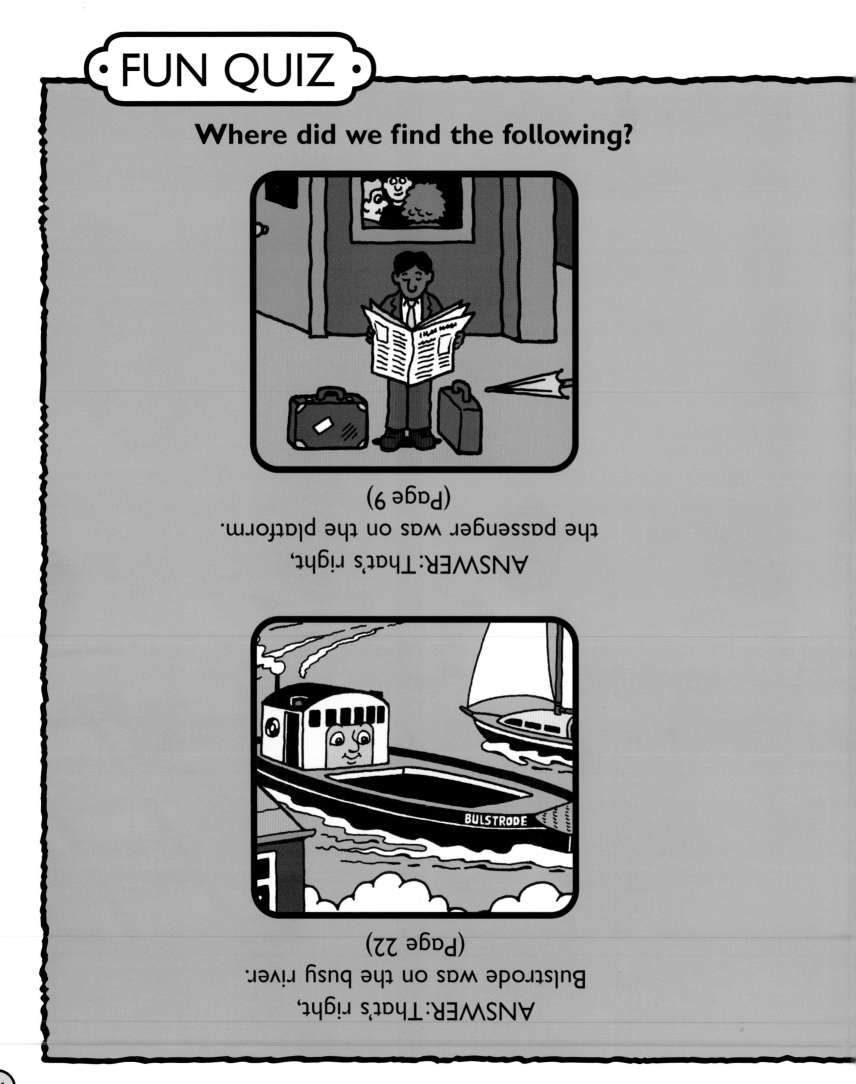

ANSWER: That's right,
the passenger was on the platform.
(Page 9)

ANSWER: That's right,
Bulstrode was on the busy river.
(Page 22)

ANSWER: That's right,
the zebra was in the wildlife
park. (Page 19)

ANSWER: That's right,
the fish tank was at the school.
(Page 16)

·FUN QUIZ·

Where did we find the following?

ANSWER: That's right,
the boy was on the beach.
(Page 39)

ANSWER: That's right,
the candyfloss and coconut stall
was at the funfair. (Page 24)

ANSWER: That's right,
the man was on a picnic.
(Page 14)

ANSWER: That's right,
the sheepdog was on the
farm. (Page 42)